Romancing the Divine

POETRY by the MYSTIC RIVER

Jacqui Lalita

ISBN: 1-4392-6362-0

ISBN-13: 9781439263624

Table of Contents

Introduction

This is a night flight to Venus, a sweeping tour of the Earth, a tango to the moon... a journey inward and upward. These are my soul's songs of remembrance, passionate proclamations to sip the sweet nectar of each moment of our wild lives. These poems have all been written recently in a blaze of spontaneous creation. Many years and lifetimes of being a loyal student to the plant teachers and stars and an ardent observer of human life has delivered me to deep mystic rivers of inspiration. Passion pulses through my veins, undulates within my hips, and throbs across my fingers to meet you in these pages. May this humble offering of poetry help remind us to dance, celebrate and be kind to each other as we walk this good Earth together as one human family.

Love in all ways,
Jacqui

An Invocation to All My Relations

Because prayer is everywhere
and the likeness of Great Spirit
is to be found in all things,

This is a humble offering of loving intent
that we all may find our wings...

To the four corners of our world
rising sun of the East,
Earth guardians of the South,
water devas of the West,
wind spirits of the North,

To rhythms and cycles, circles of completion, the round Earth,
to returning to the Source from which we've come,

To the radiant and awakened soul alive inside all creatures,
To the winged ones, the swimmers, the four-leggeds,
the creepy crawlers, giant beasts, stone people and mighty trees

To the air and space that surrounds all form,
To Mother Earth and Father Sky,

To our ancestors and great ones who have walked before us
To our descendants carrying us inside their bones
To our unborn souls waiting to take form,
To our dying ones waiting to fly
To all native people and cultures
who preserve a way of life
worth living

This is a written prayer to the seen and unseen
and all places in between

A Prayer that we may remember,
the essence of Great Spirit
alive inside all things,

Through the purity of loving thoughts and words
we find there lies our wings.

Mystical Mandalas by Sarah Greene
www.ordered-chaos.com

Book cover design by Malcom Davis
www.behance.net/anzaazul

Interior design by Walton Mendelson
www.12on14.com

Dedication

For Riley, my best friend and furry muse
whose unconditional love inspires me
to sing the praises of Heaven on Earth.
Our souls shall forever snuggle.

Others Like Me

There are others out there like me.
People too sensitive for this world
who stay up too late with books and music
and friends
and the moon
and anything that makes them cry.

There are people who love their dog so much
and keep confusing him with God,
people who find the air erotic
and pass their nights in the company of wind.

There is a woman who wants to love a man forever
but is terrified of her own annihilation,
who runs in and out of half loves
seeking solace with the wolves

And a man who yearns to be held by woman
to return to his mother's womb
and be stitched together again with love
piece by piece to be born anew.

There are lovers who want to know each other
since before they were born
To somehow have their hearts woven together
from another world

And they are out there
stumbling and searching for each other
in the eyes of strangers

People who want to love someone so deeply
but are still remembering how.

There are others out there like me
who want to know, taste and touch this whole world
Dreamers and believers in destiny
who tatter between awe of the great mystery
and an overwhelming sensitivity to it

Modern people still rooted in the ancient ways
who see that song and spirit are everywhere
who deepen their breath and notice
someone else there watching over.

There are others like me
opening little doors to this new day
to find the sun and blue sky
and vibrant fearless flowers
have come through for us once more.

Spiral Dance

Surely you have longed for it...
that limitless presence of God
to come and hold you through dark nights

You've read a lot about him
even deciding for certain that he is a he
though in fact, the Great Mother was once
worshipped by millions attuned to her cycles

You've talked about the concept,
cogitated over ideas and esoteric philosophies
submitted to detailed lists of commandments
about what thou shall and shall not do

But have you seen God
in the snowflakes,
in the grass,
in the ancient armor of sea turtles?

Have you felt the spiral of your own DNA
matching that of our spiraling galaxy?

Have you felt the dust of stars on your lips
breathing their fragrance through your words?

Have you closely examined autumn's leaves
as pages of a sacred text containing
answers to everything?

Or do you continue to wait,
longing for proof and postulations
praying for salvation
staying blind to the blinding beauty,
scouring you life for signs of God

while everything around
and within you
does its spiral dance...

Morning Prayer

From the high hillside of this heavenly new day
I see the million ways we kneel down to pray...

I see yogis on mats stretching limbs to the sky
an elder's last breath and a newborn's first cry
majestic hawks circling in freedom above
and soft songs emanating from the lips of love

I see early morning lovers coming closer to share
the scent of spring jasmine floating on air

I smell fruits and roots and spices and grain
being stirred together to cure our pain
I see sculpting and weaving and art that inspires
drumbeats shaking our hips around fires

I see babies and breasts and the mother's embrace
drenched in the light and showered by grace

I feel the sun's lips kissing our skins
and the gravity of stillness as this wild Earth spins
The planets orbiting us for billions of years
and the oceans spilling with our salty tears

I hear stories being passed from one to the other
and I look upon all as a sister or brother

From the high hillside of this heavenly new day
I see the million ways we kneel down to pray.

Flower of Life

allows for feeling of safety like that of the womb

Flower of Life

Night blooming jasmine wove a flower of life
web across the stars
transporting you to Venetian shores
by way of Mars
You arrived tangled in tendrils
sweet smelling blooms
slippery and wet
fresh out of her womb

I combed your hair
bathed your skin
twirled you into a portal spin
expansive and soft, explosive and still
a floral nectar drip inside of each thrill
succulent and sweet with a heavy sigh
spring orgies blossomed throughout the sky

Descending depths, ascending heights
our portal was a borderless city of lights
where again and again,
you fell under her spell
seduced in the night by jasmine's smell
she stripped you naked
tangled your hair
and the night blooms perspired
for having you near.

A Moon Myth

Moon drenched she emerged in a silvery hue
casting her radiance on all those she knew
and all those who loved her came closer to swoon
as her ripe breasts shimmered fleshy masses of moon

Her endless locks cascaded down to her waist
and her cinnamon scent made them all mad for her taste
the wild curves of hips and her soft supple belly
turned the knees of her watchers into tubs of jelly...

Collapsing down on the grass she spread her legs wide
and felt sure she could fit the whole world inside
She felt the moon enter and penetrate her so deep
a river sutra of rapture that made her heart weep
Vulnerability danced inside climatic surprise
as the sacred gates opened between her thighs...

Legs to the sky pointing straight overhead
she had come here to die
on her virgin deathbed

And the moon devoured her in one swift bite
where she remains eternally
shimmering flesh of light.

Intoxication

Whose tavern is this I enter before dawn,
Whose sky that I circle with golden eagles?

I am drunk without a sip to drink
full without a bite to eat
intoxicated by love without my lover's lips on mine

I threw everything I had out the window
the night you came
including myself

Now I am homeless
yet home alas
naked, clothed only in compassion

Empty yet overflowing,
wandering the gardens late at night
falling to my knees
weeping at the sight of tansies.

Mystic Milk

She had two stars for nipples
two wild moons for breasts
and a spiraling galaxy of comets
made up all the rest,

Her braids were woven rainbows
her lips were glistening gold
She was a creature born of stardust
an enigma to behold

Her dress was made of purple petals
her necklace made of bones
In heightened arousal she meandered
the world
moaning in low tones...

Her hips swayed like twilight's
river slinking spells
across the dusk, impregnating
the air with longing
for her seductive
starry musk...

Her voice was sweet as honeydew
floating in on silk
and from her starry nipples
she excreted mystic milk

Her milk carried all the wisdom
since the first human had arrived
Within her DNA the Akashic
Records all survived...

Come closer for a sip, she beckoned
as her followers came near
And one by one they sipped from the starry nipples
of this wild seer

I myself drank from her breast
and felt my whole body split in two
as the luminous love and light of Heaven
at once come pouring through!

My bones then turned to shining crystals
My blood became the sea
With every sip of her sweet milk
My heart came bursting free,
Until I too returned to stardust
and two moons became my breasts
and a spiraling galaxy of comets filled in all the rest

And now I carry mystic milk
with double helix information,

And myself and every woman alive
hold the secrets of creation...

Each woman is a starry mystic
with hips that hypnotize
Come closer for a sip, she beckons
with comets in her eyes

And here come thirsty men
who yearn to sip
from her sweet moon
Giving her the sacred seeds to sow
star children in her womb

With hair of woven rainbows
and lips of glistening gold
Every woman is a stardust creature
an enigma to behold
an enigma to behold.

Regeneration

I believe music and dancing can save the world.
It has saved my soul on many nights, and now

when the pages turn and the body quivers and burns
writhes in despair,
poetry whispers across thin air

I am a woman made of blood and tears
witnessing the way days melt into years
Falling in love, being reckless with hearts
dodging the bulls eye in the game of darts

My regenerative forces are alive and strong
and each tender upset births new song
and every wrong turn and presumed missed chance
awakens depths within my dance
Each day uprooted without a home
spins tired ache into a poem

Self love must arrive to hold one first
quenching all of longing's thirst
Devotion to one's art must follow
dare not postpone until tomorrow

The world may turn us upside down
shatter us from root to crown
but still there is the one who came to taste
this life of flavors, dare not waste
the aching or the burn on fear
for always... all ways
art is near.

Avatars of the Ocean

Lemurian myths say there are avatars
in the sea, dolphins and whales
from the Sirius constellation
here to teach us

———◆———

In the magic hour before dawn
I found myself,
in their eternal ocean of existence
riding magnificent breaths within
underwater whale songs

An ancient orca offered me a grand tour
on her back, circumambulating
deep sea wonder worlds
across the Pacific and up through the Atlantic
telepathically telling me
"We are the vibrational stewards of Planet Earth
here to remind humans
of the wisdom they hold
in their spirit bodies"

With that she came smashing through
the surface of the sea
her slippery mass tossing me
into the air to land
with a jolt on my motionless bed

———◆———

And I have known what it is to live...
as a big Buddha whale
inveterate composer of the sea
throbbing with song
gliding my tonnage
as though it were weightless
pulsing with poetry
free

What bashful words might I offer
to their ineffable songs
avatars of the ocean
I have fallen silent
awe-struck in
devotion

Remember Love

"This sky where we live is no place to lose your wings so love, love, love." — *Hafiz*

See God in everything
Goddess in every face
Let every interaction today
be kissed by the lips of Grace

From the One to the Many
the Many back to the One
remember to look up this morning
to salute our radiant Sun...

and gaze up to the sky tonight
to that full moon shining bright
Remember our truth, our destiny
to turn back into light...

Acknowledge all the star creatures
hovering earnestly above
in every blessed breath
remember...
You Are Love

Sacred Quiver

Surrender to the scintillating scent of sensuous love
who tears your robes off under the glow of moon and sun
Oh whole and holy one spinning naked across the night
light my soul on fire
ignite desire of a primal kind
beyond the mind, this piping flesh and throbbing heart
now where to start...
one soft kiss and then another
divine lover on this mystic beach
reach into my soul with tender eyes
between my thighs there lies a river
sweet life giver whose sacred quiver shall reveal
there is no place love cannot heal

Whirling Dervish

Turning towards ecstasy I become you
my body becomes the Earth's axis spinning
across cyphers of spiraling light
as I lift my arms setting ten thousand
white doves loose to fly

Every rotation is a prayer for peace
every spin a revelation
of oohs and aahhs, I am the melodies of stars
the merging of light and form
the calm inside tempestuous storm

I tip my head and bow
to the wind's reticent whispering
to be here now

I don't know how I came to be
this dervish dancing ever free
burning in the center of love's wildfire
turning towards ecstasy ascending higher and higher

One day I simply lifted my right palm to the Heavens
and offered my left palm to the Earth
and began to whirl across incarnations
spinning life, death, rebirth.

A love this great must be shared!
I shout out to a passerby
who regards me with a curious eye

A love this great must be shared!
I keep proclaiming again and again
until every who, what, why and when

reflects a sacred mirror for all to see
I become ecstasy as you become me

My dervish skirt reaches towards heaven's sky
setting ten thousand white doves loose to fly.

Kali's Invitation

You've been calling to me...

I am goddess of creation
dark mother of the night
dancer of death and destruction

I shatter
delusions of self with my bloodstained sword

I swallow
you and all beings who desire
annihilation into my formlessness

I spark
a serpent up your spine that explodes
into a thousand petaled lotus crown

I spin
your very existence upside down
so you may drown in my potent river

I am Life giver
offering sips of ambrosia
from my heavy breasts

I am ocean of blood
feasting upon primordial flesh
from which all life has come

I float on jasmine tendrils through the air
shooting shards of wisdom from my hair

I am your womb and your tomb

spinning an eternal cycle of life death life
shredding you to pieces with my holy knife

I heard you, tender lover,
calling on me
asking to take all that is not free

You whispered my name, contemplated
my form, now
I double dare you to enter my storm.

Devotion

assists in keeping the heart and mind open and devoted to thoughts and actions of the highest good

Ambition

Do you ever sit down with stiff brow
to examine your life and wonder
what on Earth are you doing

How do the days pass so quickly?
Where went those spellbound nights
in the arms of new love?
What became of those small fortunes amassed
through your past labors?
How did you arrive in this moment
naked, hungry, lost at sea?

———•———

The past is a dream ship sailing by
The future is a trickster pirate luring you
to promised treasures
Your life is in between them
in the center of the ocean's depth
Any direction you swim shall lead to
somewhere

The dolphins taught me this much:
Celebrate more, worry less
spend the spark of life on this moment
Make your living an ocean of joy.

There is a tender unrest within that cannot be quelled
a latent stirring of divine discontent
that keeps us reaching higher

Is there alas an island of ultimate fulfillment
in the stormy sea of passion and purpose?

The dolphins don't seem to be searching for it.
While we humans sit with furled brows
wondering what to make of our lives
they are painting art across the sunsets
knowing there is always reason enough
to leap for the joy of living.

The Way Home

When vulnerability opens the tear gates
and I walk the streets alone
through empty crowds of strangers
all searching for our way home

When sweet lips of yesterdays
fade into solemn nights
and the woo of unknown lands
sends me fleeing city lights

When dark long roads and shaky buses
twisting and turning with desire
deliver me in shattered pieces to the shores
of longing's fire

When I cannot be invisible
when I'm followed where I go
when I decline again and again
but nobody hears my no

When their eyes are filled with hunger
and my form becomes their prey
my breath is short, my aching long
from all this running away

When I've sailed through skies and seas
traversing oceans wide
When the sun and moon and stirring wind
has been my only guide

When apathy devours passion
my belly is left to growl
and burning tears burst forth
inside a moonlit midnight howl
When the Orient Express drops me off at a locked gate
and patience ditches me at the entrance
insisting she can't wait

When I am queasy from roaring motors
weaving through towering peak
my soul begs for me to answer
What does this seeker truly seek?

When I drown myself in dreaming
vulnerability becomes my song
and the road on this night train
grows bittersweet and long

When the other side of freedom
smacks me hard across the face
I feel myself falling into the void of infinite space

When my senses become numb
and all colors fade to black
I crawl onto the dirt and beg the Earth
to take me back

In the warmth of her embrace
her throbbing strength to persevere
all at once I remember
Now the reason why I am here...

A soft petal of a woman
so vulnerable on her knees
spilling tears to send the rivers ebbing and flowing into seas

Traversing all of this wild planet
on a street car called alone
Sinking my feet into the soil
Remembering...

The Earth is my way home

Legacy of Love

There is a Universe that never stops offering its magnificence,
A life that keeps going long after we vanish

We sleep at night while a million stars keep winking at us
We close our lips but the soul's song continues...

On the island of Bali
there is no word for art or artist
Hand carved temples line the streets
as ornately costumed dancers
move to the primal calls of Gamelan music

Each day trays of fresh fruits are piled high
and served to the Gods with sticks of sweet burning incense

To the Balinese art is not a job or hobby
It is a way of life
The entire island is full of artists
Who have no name for art
Who pass the days creating beautiful things
to blanket the island in their devotion

When your bones turn to dust
what beauty will you leave behind?
Let love be your legacy
and when your lips close
your soul's song will continue singing

Create something beautiful today...
Be a lover and an artist and offer everything
to this life you've been born into
to this Universe that never stops
offering its magnificence

Let each stroke of your paint brush,
each pluck of your guitar
each line and each note
be an offering
to the life that prevails
long after we vanish.

Lost Love Remembered

There was that one I let slip away...
and tonight, looking out at the moonlight
shimmering atop the ocean
I keep thinking

of his form,
his perfect dark features
his deep voice and the songs he used to sing
the way he brought a million gifts and smiles
to each day

That one I let slip away...
I wasn't ready or so I told myself
and there were so many ships in my sea
so I remained elusive while he burst with love for me

True there are always more
lips to kiss
more bodies to press against
more souls to journey with...

But you know how it is when that one
leaves his footprint in your heart
no others seem to fill?

He's somewhere on this wide Earth
singing to the moon
serenading the shimmering sea
and I can hear his voice across the latitudes
wrapping itself around me

Life is a slippery place
When the perfect love drops from the sky
cover their soul in kisses and love them by and by

Surrender

was drawn in contemplation of a life dedicated to service

Good Medicine

*"The human race has only one really effective weapon,
and that is laughter."* — *Mark Twain*

We laughed from morning, day to night
nibbling on the wisdom of chocolate light

We undulated out poetry in a creation story
and laughed our hearts into a blaze of glory

We sat ourselves down with the Divine
as our awakened souls poured wine

We dipped our spoons into laughing bowls
gorging giggles to our joyous souls

Celebrating, dancing, feeling merry and fine
pleasing the Gods from our sacred silly shrine

And still we're laughing as I write this poem
from the land of laughter we call home

And all these words are stamped with bliss
sent inside a giggling kiss

The best remedy to chase all maladies away:
One heaping spoonful of laughter
taken generously throughout each day.

Spreading Wings

Wild Woman walks a winding road
weaving wisdom into whimsical whirls of wonder
for every moonstruck night and the great Light within.

She laughs, she cries, she dies each night
to be reborn at dawn
singing her praise for the many ways this Life
never ceases to amaze.

Wild woman with your heart set free
shall we dance inside our destiny?
and how about let go and surrender all,
relinquishing the need to ever play small.

Force of nature one with all things
wild woman simply spread your wings

Falling Into Grace

We all need to fall down sometimes.
I too have fallen to find my whole world
turned upside down in an instant

It could be that falling down is God's ineffable way of raising us up
in faith and fortitude, realness and resilience
It could be that falling down is a miracle in itself,
that all the small and great ways we are challenged
teach us about getting up, brushing the dust off our bruised, broken bones
and beginning anew.

When I teach Sufi dervish whirling, the first thing I demonstrate is how
to fall down how to surrender to the ground,
then once the dizziness has passed,
how to get up and enter the dance again

However we fall down it is always an opportunity for transformation
Many great artists, healers and visionaries have taken huge falls
and learned what it is to rise by trial and fire.
We could say that falling down and getting up is one way we are guided
back to our innermost being, to rise in humble glory again and again.

The Wilderness Within

A tale from the depths just beneath our skin
from a wild land called the wilderness within...

From outer space to inner space, where galaxies reside
Inside our mystery secret worlds hide

Subatomic particles and cosmic dust
conjoin inside a fiery lust
Soul gardens bloom with redolent flowers
as life prevails across the hours

ten thousand miracles inside every beat
ten thousand steps daily
from two humble feet

A liver, life giver, a sweet tooth, a spleen
Bones, brains, and blood a splendiferous team

Pulsations of pleasure, an orgasmic rush
Volcanic eruptions from an island so lush

Tastes and touches and looks and feels,
The million secrets our skin conceals

Fingers and toes bristling with Sun
Carved by creation from the hands of the One

This perfect vessel merging liquid and light
Each quantum piece fitting together just right

An unfathomable tale just beneath our skin
A wild land of perfection
Our wilderness within

My Greatest Teacher

There are those great teachers worth crossing the oceans.
Many times I have
boarded planes and rickety buses for a chance
to sit at the feet of such living masters

There are those great teachers worth their weight in gold
Many times I have
given all my emeralds and rubies for a moment
to hear the masters speak

There are saints whose benevolence sings
seers who soar on wizard wings
shamans whose medicine songs inspire
and masters who've shown me original fire

So many oceans and deserts crossed
countless fortunes made and lost
months and years spent chasing tails
for the hope that unbound love prevails

After all the workshops, retreats, cold nights
passed at the guru's feet
bookshelves full of postulations, upside down 3 am meditations,
Tantra, the Tao and a worn out copy of Be Here Now
So many great teachers I have known
but to find the greatest of all here at home...

Tucked up in a little ball uttering little happy sighs
every lesson I ever needed shining
from those melty eyes

He embodies devotion, loyalty, pure joy and presence.
He offers gratitude for every meal,

practices forgiveness regularly,
takes time to smell the roses
and the rosemary and lilies too.

He asks for so little and gives so fully...

I arrive home from dizzying journeys to kneel
at the paws of my greatest teacher
who nuzzles his warm head on my lap
wags his tail in wild abandon
and begins once more to teach me
the many things he knows
about unconditional love.

Heart Seduction

In the darkness where I was born,
through early morning hours of longing,
I knocked on your holy door again

I sang you the ancient names
praying for some mystic hour to strike down
and plunge me into the golden depths

In the hushed moments of night
when the innerness of all life
began to hum as one
I felt you drawing near

I wanted to be strong enough
to bear your immense love upon my shoulders
I wanted my voice to be 108 angels
welcoming you in,
and though I could not sing too beautifully,
I began once more
to dance for you

It was you who taught me the art of heart seduction
where channels of light are sent onto another
and two breaths merge to sip together
from the liquid crystals of your holy fountain

There I was in the dark,
seducing you to become you,
with a hope,
that I might one day walk in this world,

across widening rainbows of light
through mystic hours, and ordinary ones,
seeing your ancient face hiding everywhere
knowing you are with me.

Unity

*allows for attunement to the oneness of all things transcending
the appearance of space-time reality*

Forgiveness

We all have someone who has served us
a double scoop of injustice
Who has trampled over our hearts
manipulated our minds,
someone who has wanted more than we could give

Teachers come in a myriad of forms
my enemy is wearing God's face again.

We can harbor our wounds and wrongdoings
until the skies are camouflaged in gun smoke
and twenty million are dead from famine
but we can't stop the sun from shining
or alter the divine order of things

This Universe is conspiring for our evolution
Sometimes a messenger is sent
to deliver a lesson our soul needs

A taunting tyrant knocked on my door once or twice
always in the strangest hours
No tea and honey could quell the crazed look
in his twisted eyes as he pillaged my quietude
and splattered red rage across my ceilings

None of this is ever personal.

We all want to get what we want
and want what we get
Control is a futile beast.

And now,
there is a madman in my kitchen
guzzling my finest wine from the bottle
leaving shattered glass beside my bed

I want to keep everyone happy all the time
but there is only one set of bones I can own.

Sometimes we are messengers
who teach each other about heartbreak

Let each feel what they need to feel
let the decibels in their voices rise to feverish pitch
let the walls of this old house be a quivering witness

When the bones where we reside have spilled their sorrow
still there is a sunrise awaiting us

Last night's tyrant is today's package on the doorstep
I examine the neatly wrapped box with its big red bow
shaking it up to my ear
I have seen this gift before:

    Forgiveness.

Says the Soul

I have known this Earth before...
its familiar scent and wild beauty
its paradise coves and mighty waterfalls
its suffering and hardship, its heartache
and starvation
its oceans of loss and separation
its web of life and interconnectedness
its learning and lessons
all pointing back to Love...

I have forgotten and remembered
the great truth of life and death

We are all immortal!

On this familiar Earth I have died
at least 2000 times

As a priestess in the Temple of Amun
a peasant farmer in Palestine
an Incan medicine woman
a nurse for the Spanish army
a tribesman of early America

I lived and died on both sides of slavery
both sides of justice
both sides of power and gender...

I have been in so many bodies
but only one soul...

Many of us have been together before
Traversing centuries as they were minutes

Playing teachers and students for each other
Evolving and dissolving back into Light...

Could you believe that we are Eternal....

On Receiving

Rain in the mountains is a holy experience

Every tree and plant opens
their throats to sip in
Earth's celestial elixir
drenching and quenching,
dryads, fairies, keepers of the hills,
sacred sagebrush spirits all smudged
in curative cloud waters

Distant homes take on romantic loneliness
Chimney smoke paints songs of seclusion
and human life retreats inside the nebulous mist

Here appears a clarity too intimate
for sunny days,
Who waits patiently
for the mountains and her creatures to become submissive

Then showers us
with her holy message,
Receive...
Receive...
Receive...

Her drops fall with tender thuds upon the land
and we are all
made new again.

Naked in Nature

Naked in nature
with bare limbs against sycamores
winding through whimsical woods
on an untold road to
nowhere...

The winds of spontaneity
blowing through my bones
leaping from stone to stone
My hair wildly free...
My heart wildly free...
Every quantum piece of me
Free as free can be.

Who said all this living had to be so serious?

May I propose
you swiftly find yourself
Naked in nature
Succumbing to the simple sensation
of being penetrated by the midday sun

Listening to the ruffle of the trees
stirring the breeze between your knees...

There is no shame in sensuality ~

We came into this world without clothes
and soon enough we shall return
to the sweet mists of Avalon
whose dew rises to kiss all naked skins...

There is an Earth so sensual
who yearns to know you
Lay your limbs down upon her
Breathe into her
and behold your true nature
as a sensuous creature
born naked on this wild land.

Stepping Up

The day will come
when excuses no longer suffice
that old dusty dream will tumble down
from the closet to clobber you in the head

As you lay there entangled
in spider webs
you will have no choice
but to break free from the stories
that have kept your truth enslaved
and the days passed hauling
your heartache around like a lame leg.

The day will come
when you will choose to shine
and offer your wildest dream up
to the Great One

who, as it turns out,
will be doing half of the work for you

Joy

Once upon a time we walked barefoot upon the Earth
sharing an unspoken understanding
that to sing at dawn and to dance at dusk
was to heal the broken pieces
of ourselves and our world
with joy.

Wherever we are in this moment
with whatever problems weigh upon our hearts

Let us go forth remembering
what we may have forgotten
what the animals and plants remind us daily
That our life is meant to be celebrated
and our days meant
to be danced with joy

*allows for the concept of heaven on earth to
be felt within the heart and mind*

Ambrosia

Crackling embers consummate
another ambrosial night

Friends cozy around the fire
Sharing music and morsels
Celebrating the good fortune
of knowing each other

This life being
exactly what life is for.
Could any heart want more?

Our resplendent laughter and music
billowing out in a blanket of joy
floating across the sleeping beach
down chimneys, through window cracks
Tickling and caressing tender backs

Nibbling on dreaming ears
evaporating worries and tears
till all the town is dreaming sweet
rising and falling to our drumbeat

All the hearts filled to the rim
as our blazing fire begins to dim

And our music and laughter trickles down
to crackling ember's abating sound

A cozy pile of friends and food
can circulate a winsome mood
gently knocking on each and every
neighbors door to remind them
what this life is for.

Desert Spell

She casts her spell across seething sands
setting souls and skins on fire
and we all become the Phoenix rising
from the ashes of our desire

Dreams melt inside of days and turn mystic by the night
Starlight spreads its glory across her sky
to bathe our primal sight

She carries wisdom in on wind
of ancient cultures and lands
dusting us with the ashes of lovers
scattered across her sands

We sip her wine of stillness
getting drunk on revelation
as she aligns our channels
to the pulse of Source creation

Shooting stars sweep over us
as the desert comes alive
and for a moment
in this spellbound land...
We all begin to thrive

Lands of Innocence

I know some days on this journey of life
it can feel hard to put one foot in front of the other

I know sometimes all our longing and yearnings
can feel too heavy a weight to bear...
But remember when you were a child
skipping through the woods
with the sun's rays on your skin

Remember when you were wild and free
and felt like you could do anything?

I want to meet you in the golden sun and run with open arms
    across those lands of innocence...
I want to hold your hand and dance our footprints of Joy
upon this Earth

And maybe others will hear our laughter being carried on the wind
    and remember
there was a time they too felt like they could do anything

And it is still here now

All One

Twilight's thick fog
wraps itself around me
on the loneliest
most romantic night
I've ever known
Vanishing into the Pacific
all alone

Barefoot and free
Running through the purple fog
of dusk
Inhaling negative ions soaked
in ocean's musk
1001 miles away
from all the lips I've ever kissed
Liberated at once
from all the arms I've ever missed

Here and only here
a woman running with the wolves
Howling wildly into the night
Soaring with my totem owl
on feathered wings of light

Taking fog as my tender lover
Lapping waves as my foreplay
Forgetting every fleeting love I've had
before today

Making sweet love to the Mystery
Every breath begets a poem
Vanishing into infinity
All one
Alone

New Moon Lunacy

She entrances us in lunacy
Every inhalation
Breathes revelation...

Whispering with reticence,
She spins in golden rhythmic ciphers
Revealing ancient remembrance

Healing long forgotten places,
She traces our curves
in the dark night,
Shining light upon desire
Igniting a fire that kindles
below our waist
Her taste is wild honey
inspiring us to blossom and bloom
to strip off old layers and dance in the nude

She sings beguilingly across the sky
come, gather your greatness
clearly state your desire
and throw all appetence
into the loin of her fire

Plant your dream seeds as the new moon is born
while she coos and woos and we all sing
her song of lunacy.

Law of the Cosmos

Many faces and many moods
of our night sky Goddess
Dear loyal moon

Timekeeper, mirror of the Sun
Aligning biorhythms
to the One

High and low she draws the sea
dangling in arcane mystery

Lifter of oceans
Her invisible force renders life infallible
when she's void of course,

All-seeing witness cloaked in compassion
wearing every face in flawless fashion

She vanishes sometimes behind her veil
to reemerge on a deep inhale

Her seduction swells across the sky
enthralling every watching eye

She sends poets writing,
Artists painting,
Lovers looking
for new romance

The whole wide world goes wild
as we slip under her lunar trance

And so it reads
a cosmic law, in stardust
all across the sky:

"Thou shall dance under our Mother Moon
with reverence every night until you die"

Crossroads

*allows for ease with major life changes and
assists with decision making*

Crossroads

And then there came a crossroads...
a familiar beaten path splitting suddenly to reveal
some wild call from deep within the soul
which you had silenced,
but still came on cold nights
singing through taped up lips to haunt you

And there stood the two of you
that old familiar one who tugged and pleaded
to turn back and play things safe
and that new one, who had in fact been there
all along, whose voice had grown
too loud to ignore

However big or small your life
a crossroads had found you
and there you stood at the intersection of fate and free will
seeing the many bad choices you had made
opportunities missed for overly lengthy deliberations
fortunes lost for hasty maneuvers
true love forsaken to spare the tender heart from opening

And this moment where you now stood
choosing to walk with chin high towards your dreams
the future singing her ancient song of the unknown
as songs of the past
that no longer moved you
began to fade away under the shadows
of oak trees

whose branches stretched wide across you
offering answers and explanations
to everything.

Supernova Lover

You make a girl want to leave her feminine
flesh and bones to soar
the bioluminous sphere
to be there, surfing on you
whispering these words in your ear:

You love the ocean
You love my skin
Where does one end
and the other begin?

There are waves when I'm yours
when I want to keep diving in
and sometimes a wave
when I belong to the wind...

If love is the way God's secrets get told
I'll dive into these waters
courageous and bold

As the unseen goes seen
the pathways in between
reveal themselves through lucid dream

You come to me when I sleep whispering grace
Singing love knows no limits of time and space
I awaken soaked in tidal pools of desire
Teleporting to you in a flash of fire

Somewhere in the galaxy in this moment
a supernova star is exploding into existence
and poof!!
I am here with you

Spinning under the stars
exploding into existence
whirling supernova lovers
Belonging only to the wind.

A Blazing Life

Yesterday it hit me again
the fragility of this giant force of life

The long days and nights of ambition
dreaming and dancing on moonlit rooftops
that can end in an instant.

I know a man who lived the life of a dozen men
across thirty blazing years
His laughter used to soar above the desert sky
as we drove in his old pickup
pueblo to pueblo singing love ballads,
under shooting stars,
believing ourselves invincible.

It was hard to imagine we would not be here forever
in this life we had come to know so well

Then when he died
four days before his thirtieth birthday
wrapped in passion's tourniquet
I thought about all the hearts, like mine, he had touched
and all the wild nights, like ours,
he had thrown his arms out to the sky
to behold the beauty of a single moment

And that one fragile moment
when all that he knew
fell silent around him.

We ought to treat this life as a force
a very mighty and fragile force
that can come like thunder
or strike us down like lightening

We ought to let our laughter blaze
from pueblo to pueblo
shining like flashes
of shooting stars across the desert sky
lighting up as many nights as we are given
until the darkness comes to claim us.

Prophecy

Lakota, Hopi, Navajo
Guarani, Cofan, Shipibo
Berber, Zulu, Tuareg, Maasai
Huichol, Maori, Kutenai

Children of the Incan Sun
Remembering Now...
The dream of One

Ancestors who knew to fly
Dreamtime weavers in the sacred sky
Ancient ones with wings to soar
Opening hearts to Heaven's door

The elder council always knew
their prophecies would soon come true
A tribe of rainbow warriors across all lands
would circle together holding hands

Our future leads us to our past
to the wisdom ancient tribes amassed
Back to the land, to the ritual and story
to a time of paradise when the Earth
was in her glory

We stand here now with hearts united
all colors, creeds, and skins
as prophecy spreads feathered wings
a new dawn on Earth begins

Mimes

My Mimes is my hero

At 4′9″ she is the smallest woman I look up to
I watch her pushing ninety years of stories around
on her walker
carrying her little life with pride.

She married a brilliant mind who
was there but never there,
raised three children on her own
taught herself to drive in the 1950s
enduring many raised eyebrows
as she barreled down the residential streets of Boston

Every summer for decades she traveled alone
to the Amazon jungle to visit our family
Once guerilla terrorists kidnapped her for weeks
Upon release she shrugged her little shoulders
and said the experience wasn't half bad.

All the seniors where Mimes lives in Rhode Island
have crowded into the room
in hushed anticipation for my dance show

I survey the crowd of fluffy white heads
and when I spot my Grandmother
this tiny woman overflowing with love, lessons,
grace and gratitude, sitting quietly with her walker
and a smile stretched ear to ear
I know I've got to keep going like this
making each moment of this little life
something to smile about in the end.

Insomnia

The full moon presses herself against my skin
There is no sleep for me tonight as fires burn
across this city of angels
I am on fire
The whole world is on fire
Everywhere I turn, fire...

I rip off my clothes and flee to the silent streets of 5 am
and begin to scream for the dolphin slaughterings in Japan
the genocide in Darfur,
for my brothers and sisters in Afghanistan,
the oil pipelines pillaging Amazon tribes,
factory farming destroying our native seeds,
for all the wild majestic beasts held in captivity,
for the innocent ones locked in cement cages...
for the wild minds of my generation
trapped in mental slavery...

This is a powerful time to be alive
We ought to smile at each other more
See the Holy Spirit in each earthly form
and help each other along the best we can...

The full moon blazes across the inferno of Los Angeles
where there are so many sleeping bodies full of sludge
and this one loony naked woman
running up and down the streets
screaming for everyone to wake up.

Common Ground

We all dream under the same moon and build our
houses on the dirt
We've put our faith and hope in the Great Mystery...
Given so many names to Spirit:
Allah, Buddha, Krishna, Yahweh, Jehovah, God, Goddes...
Tell me which name is worth killing for

The holy day has come to lay down our swords
and pray together
To gather on the vast temple of the Earth
Kneel down or whirl
Read from the Old Testament or the Qu'ran
Sing 1000 names to God in every language
at the same time
and watch a fat bellied Buddha and Jesus
come walking hand in hand
with a jolly elephant-headed God dancing behind them

These Gods we're praying to have been busy praying together
for us to learn how to get along
They've been watching us
our one giant human family
entering our little mosques, temples, churches and synagogues
saying our morning prayers and then stepping outside
to pierce each other's hearts out with our swords

This land we've been squabbling over for so long
doesn't belong to any of us really
This is the land of our Mother
who's been waiting so patiently
for us to come home...

We all sleep under the same moon
and build our houses on the dirt
We've been sharing this vast temple of Earth together
and there is room enough here
for all to sing 1000 names to God
in every language at the same time.

Acceptance

created with the desire to accept what is as it is,
and to let go of what is not

The Royal Queen

Death is a difficult thing to watch
yet within every life it exists

It will find each of us
maybe tomorrow, maybe next century

Since we do not know when the royal queen
will plant her fatal kiss upon us
why not sip each breath
like it were a holy elixir

poured from the hands of God
to be savored and celebrated

These bodies of flesh have expiration dates
but the nectar inside our hearts
that honey suckle love blossom
shall hold its sweetness for eternity

We can shutter at the word,
shriek at the sight,
then surrender alas...
Death will find us all.

And within every death
The holy nectar of our heart
shall keep us forever sticky sweet
soaring among the living.

Good-byes

He is preparing to leave
this most loyal of friends
who has made it his great duty to serve me
through sultry days in Miami
and silent nights by the Pacific

He has seen more of our country than most people
being kind to many squirrels along the way
and always looking upon the deer with reverence,

His soft fur has been touched by amazing souls
and he, with his pure heart of love, has given so much
to our world, especially mine.

He was there with me through the wild decade of my twenties
and on the morning of my 30th birthday, those brown eyes
that sing forever
serenaded me once more.

He has seen me through a dozen moves, a dozen relationships,
a dozen careers, a dozen changing dreams and fears...
and still he is here,
my best friend and protector
who, like all of us, cannot escape
the angel of death who comes without whisper or warning
making certain we all leave each other too soon

Still, I believe that death is not a going
but a changing of forms
a flight of destiny to become
everything, nothing
existence, non-existence

Can we ever really cease being?

The soul of this great dog
the soul I love so much it hurts
is ever-lasting and eternal

But here I am,
flesh clutching unto flesh
pressing his little heart against mine,
trembling at the way
I love his form.

Deliverance

There is a cold night of the soul
a river of emptiness winding through war torn lands
a window into the lives of the forlorn in the eyes I encounter

A village man passes and hits his horse aggressively
the horse looks at me to show me his eyes of despair

Desperate bony dogs comb the broken streets for crumbs
I reach out my hands to pet one, to soothe his sorrow-filled life
but he retracts and lowers his head in shame

Distrust of love is everywhere
I watch his little bones
shivering in the cold and am met with a vision
of all the suffering hungry animals of our world
who have not known the touch of a warm hand or meal

And what of the humans who suffer so deeply
who numb their souls with addictions
and wander meekly across desolate lives
without hearing the wild songs of the sparrow?

There is a river of despair that weaves
through many hearts in this world
a suffering so great it is painful to contemplate

Still, I cannot turn my gaze away from that frail dog
looking at me with his head lowered, shivering in disbelief
that I could love them

The bread I offered was barely enough to keep him alive for a few
days,
A token of hope that love may find the starving souls
of this world and offer deliverance to better days

I stand in the freezing rain watching him devour his crumbs
and realize I've got to keep praying.

Song of a Walking Giant

I dreamt I was a mighty redwood
stretching 300 feet to kiss the sky
with a soul of malleability
and an elemental wizard's eye

I became a majestic spirit
with roots woven to neighboring trees
who passed my nights under the spell of owls
sipping silence inside the breeze

I looked into the hearts of humans
held them in my embrace
asked them to remember their truth

We are born of goodness and grace

I saw visions of a time when redwoods
moved slowly upon the Earth
legends of walking giants
who shook mountains with their girth

I entered the consciousness of elementals
learned to dance inside of storm
became the confluence of roots and branches
within my sacred form

I gave the gift of oxygen
cleaned the air for life to thrive
sent my prayer out through the forest
that all species may survive

I dreamt I was a mighty redwood
soaring 300 feet to kiss the sky
who heard the sound of distant chain saws
then sang my silent cry.

Solstice Serenade

The longtime Sun stretches herself
across the sky, shining
upon the shortest day of the year

Wilderness bristles with nostalgia
Sentimentality reaches its peak
and life lingers...
somewhere between darkness and light

Eternity's cycle continues
Life-Death-Rebirth
The inhale and the exhale
Ouroboros bites his tail
and nature's recuperative spirit prevails...

Tonight Orion's belt will align
with the eastern sky's brightest star
marking the precise point
the sun will rise tomorrow

There are clues to this Mystery everywhere!
Wild trails bursting with life
Fearless creatures whose will to live is so audacious
weary limbs cant help but dance..

And so I do,
all excitable human flesh and bones
dancing with desolation
to the winter hymns of the sagebrush
whose will to keep growing through long nights
inspires a resurgence of my inner garden...

Within each of us there lives
an eternal summer
A flower of our mind's eye
whose will to shine
through the darkness
always points us back
to the light.

Crystal Passage

*allows for enhanced connection with feminine
energies and enhances sense of balance*

Body of Woman

My body is a horse
an earthly flame of force
whose fingers burn as I sing
on crashing waves and flapping wings
Behold the silent beauty of truth a woman sings

Oh woman! Your body is a Universe
existing in many spheres and dimensions
skin of silk and sand
out of the ocean you emerge dancing on the land
curves glowing in the moonlight
bringing Heaven down to Earth
Venus on her conch shell standing naked at her birth

My hips are an endless ocean
my skin a wild shore
Oh I am the body of woman! Hear me purr and roar!

A Sacred Language

We had no common words to express
so we conversed by locking lips
Sharing stories proved impossible
so I insisted he read my hips
I spoke four words in Turkish
and I made those four words dance
He knew three words in English
each dipped in sweet romance

We ran around the cobbled streets of Istanbul
then hopped onto a ferry
Kissing all across the Sea of Marmara
feeling oh so merry
He took me to an island
where we kissed the day away
and somehow without words we found
so many things to say

We spoke the language of souls
A universal ancient tongue
And together we knew all the words
To every love song ever sung

I kissed him one last time
A farewell to stretch through space
And he uttered to me a million words
From the tender look upon his face

We came from different cultures
Forming words in different ways
But for a moment we knew each other
And spoke love through a single gaze.

Dream Makers

In the forest of forgotten lands
where humans dare not tread
a fairy wrapped in autumn leaves
lay naked in her bed

A bed of cedar twigs her home
a pillow of buckwheat,
between her legs there blazed
an ancient throbbing heat

Squirming in desire
tucked alone inside the trees
she begged the cool air to consume her
as she came on hands and knees

Lost inside the rapture
sighs gave way to screams
and suddenly she found herself
by a mystic river of dreams...

The river was gushing indigo shimmering with light
the full moon dangling dangerously low
casting love spells on the night
figures wrapped in red robes huddled together sounding chimes
while others clad in all white played the role of dancing mimes

Owls hooted on branches
gallant eagles soared above
and copulating deer sang nature's song of love

Incandescent air aglow lit the fertile grounds
revealing thousands of monarch butterflies
humming sacred sounds

The giant queen of all the monarchs landed
on the faery's toe, whispering:

"We are the dream makers behind each dreaming soul...
This mystic river fortifies messages for all of those who sleep
then sends them on our glittering wings,
into the subconscious we seep

We meet you in dreamscapes each night
to help show you along
with hopes that you remember the messages
of our encrypted song

This is a land of dreams where all things are seen and known
and the message for you tonight, my dear,
you are never here alone.

The ecstasy you moan is a nourishing life giver
reverberating through the lands into this mystic river
your sighs are the nectar of sensuality that nourish all the flowers
your climax a reminder of nature's inherent powers..."

And suddenly she was back again in her little cedar bed
deep inside the pleasure that pulsed from root to head
Another land of dream-makers seen within transcendent moans
Copulating deer sighing out we are never here alone

Every climax is a ripple that reverberates near and far
Every pulsation of pleasure witnessed by a hovering star

And so this fairy smiles tonight as the forest joins along
and the world full of dreaming souls
receives the monarch's song.

Moments Alive

Curl by curl she enters
wearing the dawn on her face
smiling as she slides across the room
into your heart, and you know
how it is when someone sneaks in there

Her spirit walks through walls
and sometimes
through the fine armor of the human heart

Finger by tiny finger she dances
unwrapping seven veils to reveal
a windy curving road to Eden
the way home lit with a single smile.

She soars into the room with blessings
the floor brightens, walls awaken
stones yearn to leap through windows to
spin into non-existence at her side

When she comes to kiss you
be ready to sit erect and receive
Her lessons are greater than the day's chores
Her moments most alive.

When she comes to you
curl by curl
wearing the dawn on her face
spark that warrior candle you've been waiting to burn
and stay awake with her

Don't sleep tonight.

Invisible Support

We are never alone in this.

Many tears will be spilled across the Earth today
from bodies like ours into surging rivers
of hope

Many invisible arms will be wrapped around aching bodies,
angels who silently walk among us
will be here, as they always are
to hold us

If we could only see the ones
who surround us everyday
we would know how truly supported we are.

They hide themselves inside the deepest part of our being
ascended masters and celestial ones
residing over each breath
rooting for us to succeed in Love

The stars and oceans are rooting for us too
an Earth grounding us to her, a sky beckoning us to
reach higher, a spirit yearning to soar,
a heart begging to love without limit
We have a whole team of powerful players
on our side

And somewhere in the dust of all our seeking
we find another one who has always been there
rooting for us since the first breath

We welcome our highest self in
put the tea kettle on
and together sip in the warm truth

We are never alone in this.

Pleiades

I wandered across dark skies
in my visions to find you
guided by the light of seven shining sisters
prophets in the sky, a star system I have known
I scoured the night for my celestial roots
in a cold America on my own.

I walked many miles across farms and cities
with aching limbs and a melancholy
that throbbed within my core
I smashed stained glass windows, kicked down a temple door.

I gave my change to beggars, left my warm clothes by the stream
wandering bereft of reason across the dark skies of my dreams

Leaving friends and lovers behind
to take flight with the wind
throwing my stories into the night
to watch them all rescind

I saw wild horses soaring,
white owls taking flight
psychic pulses of creation through the eyes of primal sight

I watched a fine crumbling of reality
come galloping from the deep
awakening us once more
from a long extended sleep

I wandered dark skies in my visions
tasting freedom few have known
with seven sacred sisters
guiding me across a cold America
back to my home.

Seven Sacred Seas

I've traveled the world and the seven seas
lived inside tipis, tents and trees

floated on boats down the starlit Nile
adorning myself with a sacred smile

I've whirled with the Dervishes in Turkish lands
twirled with the Bedouins in Sinai sands

shimmied my way across sultry Spain
explored remote islands by private plane

I've swam in the Red, Dead and Mediterranean Sea
drank coconuts from the Caribbean, Indian and Jamaican tree

I've prayed with shamans, sadhus, and seers
washed away old patterns and fears

I've unlocked new dimensions with an Amazon vine
taken grand cosmic journeys and danced the divine

I've traveled the world and the seven seas
given my life to the Great Mysteries

I've known what it is to awaken and rise
to look in the mirror and see true Self in my eyes

I've died to learn the right ways to live
embodied reception to know how to give
traveled the whole world learning to sit still in one place
lived good times and hard times to find all is grace

I've awoken again as wonder's bride
slipped off my silk and stepped outside

thrown up my arms and shouted "YES! YES! YES!" to the sky
and beheld life's great secret:
Die before you die.

Passion's Proclamation

She came whirling into my life
ripping reality's seem
passionately proclaiming,

"*My child, this life is but a dream!*
While the world is stumbling sadly down an ever-fading road
take my hand in freedom and drop your heavy load
Bid farewell to illusion, relinquish thoughts of time
From this moment henceforth you shall romance the divine

The whole world is an eager lover awaiting your embrace
so shine, my child shine! Shower this existence with grace!
Dance barefoot in the rain
Let the mud caress your feet
Kiss your lover with wild abandon in the middle of the street

Take the most amazing men as lovers
the most awakened souls as friends
Stay present to every moment of life
and the beauty never ends
Live fully, Love fearlessly, Breathe deeply and be free
My child, this is your destiny!"

And since that day so long ago
of passion's proclamation
my life has been more magical than my wildest imagination

Now I come like thunder
ripping reality's seem
passionately proclaiming,
My friends, this life is but a dream!

Spread your wings, soar to the sky
make each breath count until you die
and when death's chariot draws ever near,
no lingers of remorse or fear

When you've passed your days as passion's bride
beauty stays close by your side

Lay down your burdens
Remember, you are free.
Shine my friends shine!
Live your destiny!

Passion

*allows for manifestation of creative energy and assists
in the ability to live in the moment*

The Dancer

She danced the dance of oceans aflame
she broke them with her glance,
she whirled into the hearts of many
enraptured in her trance.

She danced for all the souls who couldn't
for all the war and worlds at strife,
she tore the bondage off and leapt
for this precious chance at life,

She danced the dance to unheard melodies
moved by mystic choirs,
when the dancer doth become the dance
look how many she inspires!

Meeting Majesty

Running through misty rain
forests of silent fortitude
a romantic nostalgia reminiscent
of simpler times...

I don't want to hear about busyness
and not having enough time,
for this morning an eagle came
to tell me time does not exist

Something in the way he sailed
across the rising sun
His flight as glorious and little noticed
as many of our greatest efforts,

Something in the way his wings stretched
across an eternal sky
told me he was right

Running through misty forests
leaping over streams on limbs of light
my body and breath building the universe

Majestic steps scarcely noticed by any
but the soaring eagle who watches
and knows I've tasted eternity.

A Thousand Fires in Your Belly

When you come right down to it, all you have is yourself. Yourself is a sun
with a thousand fires in your belly. The rest is nothing. —Pablo Picasso

If you've ever wanted to touch a thousand fires within
Come dance with me tonight
let the odyssey begin...
Undulate the sun down with me
as a thousand flames ignite
Burn inside the brilliance of your radiant inner light

Dance barefoot with me here naked in the rain
and you, for this moment
shall never be the same

This ancient dance is a spiral labyrinth where hips begin to sway
across the fires of femininity a dancer finds her way...
To a time when the drummers were women
and they would shake their hips and pound
trancing themselves in ecstatic states
until their bodies hit the ground

And they would burn inside a thousand fires
to find they are the Sun
And a thousand fires in a thousand bellies
would turn back into One

Dance yourself into a trance
Burn inside your inner flame
And you, for this moment
shall never be the same

Your Self is a sun with a thousand fires in your core
Come dance with me tonight
and we shall spark a thousand more!

Harmony

invites the soul to dance with the song of Spirit

Temple of Truth

Unveiled, revealed
her form was always there
for those willing to see
her Love burns all illusions
to set the spirit free

all the searching and circumventing
desire for something higher
return to ember's dust
in the sultry
smoldering of her fire

wisdom is her nectar
passion is her wine
mysteries demystify
as bodies intertwine

evading, pervading
she graciously appears
in the stirring of your heart
and ocean salt within your tears

people are busy
scrambling for a taste
of her heavenly mousse
as you simply smile with her
she sets her silk shawl loose

keep smiling with her
as her garments come undone
she will stand before you naked
to reveal her shining sun

In a holy temple
we wild ones enter naked
each day to pray
sipping Truth's ambrosial serum
to the Heavens we are carried away.

Song of Silence

Silence took me back like she remembered me
as if all the years of noise between us
had never existed

I was home again
outstretched in the grassy arms of stillness
listening to the rhythm of my own heart beating
its perfect song

Silence remembered my scent, curves and melting spots
and with adoration she meandered across my small infinity
bowing over my bones so full of starlight and possibility

I was home again
after a long and arduous journey
through cityscapes that begged to sleep
helicopters, horns, salsa music and ringing phones
crying babies, barking dogs and barricaded construction zones

All faded into distant memories of the past
as the song of silence took me back at last

She carried me through wooded trails
into magical cedar forest groves
and floated me atop the shining sea
into the Pacific's majestic coves

She took me back like she remembered me
as if we'd never been apart
and I keep falling more and more in love
with the sacred silence in my heart.

Focus

Discipline and focus come now into my hands
Help me actualize the visions of my spirit's well laid plans
Dare not elude me today nor hide yourself tomorrow
For the deepest dreams unrealized doth fill a heart with sorrow.

Commitment and consistency teach me your great ways
Fill my spine with fortitude to spill across these days
Oh ascended ones illuminate the path
to help me move with strength
Dedication cover my lips with your empowering golden taste

Let the joy inside my heart inspire all the work I do
Oh selfless service I surrender every morsel of me to you!

There is this irresistible urge to create
A primal pulse that shall never cease
Steady focus washing over me...
Dreams realized with grace and ease.

A Beginning

So this is the end, my friend?
Or the illusion of an ending falling down like morning dew
Night surrenders darkness and the day begins anew...

That great web of life weaves interconnection with all beings
near and far, every person on this planet
every moon and falling star

Time leaps off linear planes
we close one chapter and begin another
and every moment of life's cycles
becomes a mystic lover

We came in on an inhale
Infinity knows no end...
We shall leave on an exhale
So until we meet again my friend...

A moonlit path to the lake
First kiss of love at dawn
Ripeness of summer
Music as medicine
Rebirthing, rejoicing, replenishing,
Remembering...
a little light that begs to shine
a book of secrets waiting to reveal
A wild and tender heart
that above all yearns to open

47639918R00069

Made in the USA
Charleston, SC
14 October 2015